Open Borders Behind Closed Doors

Peter Pennartz

# OPEN BORDERS BEHIND CLOSED DOORS

## The European Union and the South

International Books

edited by: Niala Maharaj
cartoons by: Peter Pennartz
drawings by: Nita Dales
cover design: Marjo Starink
cover photo: Solidaridad
printing: Haasbeek

ISBN: 90 5727 005 6
keywords: Development/ International Affairs

International Books, A. Numankade 17, 3572 KP Utrecht, The Netherlands,
telephone +31-30-2731840, fax +31 30 2733 614, E-mail i-books@antenna.nl

# Contents

# Introduction

"I sell. You buy
You sell. I buy."

Trade is an issue of everyday life. People buy and sell every day in shops and markets.
But countries, regions and continents also trade with each other. Today, more products
are crossing borders between countries than ever before. Trade is growing faster than the
production of goods. This economists say, makes everybody richer.
But some people in countries of the Third World are growing poorer every year.
Could this be linked to the growth in trade? Could it be that some people are consuming
more of the goods being traded, and getting them more cheaply, while others do without or cannot afford to buy? Who are the people that are consuming less? Do they want
to consume less? If not, why do they do it?
Imagine that you sell eggs, while your neighbour sells potatoes. Suppose your neighbour
raises the price of potatoes ten times, but refuses to buy eggs unless you drop their price
ten times. What will be the result? You will become poorer, not so?
That's the way it is with the trade between countries. But since the prices for goods at this
level are fixed, not in your local shop, but in offices far away, you don't see what goes on.
Yet the decisions on the pricing of goods, and other trade arrangements, are made in our
names. Our governments, the ones we elect, are involved. Take cigarettes, for example.
We all know that cigarette prices have gone up tremendously in Europe in the last few
years, since our governments put high taxes on them, supposedly to protect us from in-
jury to our health.
And taxes are only one of the ways governments influence trade. In the US, anyone can
buy or sell a gun. In Europe it is against the law. This is a political decision of the governments that represent us, meant to protect us from people with violent instincts. All laws
that affect the buying and selling of goods, both locally and internationally, are made to
protect us by governments acting on our behalf.

Since the evolution of the European Union (or EU), these decisions are made jointly by
Germany, France, Holland, Ireland, Great Britain, Denmark, Belgium, Luxembourg,
Spain, Portugal, Italy, Greece and recently Austria, Finland and Sweden. Having got
together as a trading group, these countries now comprise one of the largest, if not the
largest, trading blocks in the world. It has, therefore, a tremendous influence in determin-
ing who benefits by existing trade arrangements and who suffers.

And here is an example of its policies regarding people in poor countries:
The EU gives money, called "development aid", to help cattle farmers in Africa. At the same time, it gives farmers in Europe much more money, called "subsidies", to produce cattle much more cheaply. The result? European farmers export cheap beef to Africa, thereby destroying the livelihood of African cattle farmers.

Yet, according to the Maastricht Treaty, on which the EU is based:
"The Community shall take account of the objectives referred to in Article 130u in the policies that it implements which are likely to affect developing countries."
Article 130u's objectives are: "That development cooperation which shall be complementary to the policies pursued by the Member States, fostering sustainable economic and social development of developing countries, and more particularly the most disadvantaged among them, a smooth and gradual integration of the developing countries into the world economy and campaigning against poverty in developing countries."
Is the cattle example one which fosters sustainable development? Does it help in the campaign against poverty? Do any of the EU's trade policies help this campaign?

IRENE, the International Restructuring and Education Network Europe, conducted a special research project to look into this question. Together with other organisations in Europe, Latin America, Africa and Asia, we organised international workshops and seminars with activists, researchers and politicians to understand how the trade bloc called Europe affects poor people in other countries.
This book is the result.

...And since Trade is a complicated subject, we've brought into the studio Professor Sellbuy Anymeans—a European trade official—to explain the system to our interviewer, Jack Nitwit, and a studio audience.

# CHAPTER 1

# The Tools of Protection

Tariffs between most rich countries have been gradually reduced or removed. But poor countries can sell us many goods far cheaper than we can produce them, because workers there get paid little and nothing. Thus, we have to protect ourselves from them.

It's a normal, everyday practice by the EU, Japan and the USA. We rich countries make a lot of money from industry, that is, by using raw materials (cocoa, coffee etc.) from the Third World to make finished goods. And a lot more money comes from the packaging, distribution and marketing.

Look at it this way. Did you ever hear of a yuppie in Frankfurt or London going into the growing of cocoa beans? No, they go into 'careers in advertising'! Because that's where the money is made, in such services as the marketing and distribution of goods.

Lots of people in the Third World make their living producing peanuts (and cocoa beans and coffee etc). But the prices of such raw materials have been steadily dropping, so we let the raw materials in, but put high tariffs on finished goods. 70.2%, for example, on refined vegetable oil!

Between 1982 and 1984, 47% of less developed countries relied on primary products for over 75% of their exports.
But isn't this obviously against free trade?

If you're a smart producer, you dump goods on another country for a while to undersell local producers there and force them out of business. It's a very nasty practice, so there are a lot of international regulations against dumping. They're called anti-dumping measures.

These become very useful measures when you want to keep out goods from another country. Microwave ovens from Japan, Singapore and South Korea are now the subject of anti-dumping investigations. They are too cheap compared to the ones we produce! Same goes for Japanese semi-conductors and electronic scales, compact discs from South Korea and polyester fibres from Mexico, Rumania, Taiwan, Turkey, the former Yugoslavia and the USA.

Well...That's not exactly true. We 'negotiate' them into that choice.

We are strong politically. They are weak. They have to do what we say. Many Third World countries depend on us for aid, for military protection, etc. South Korea, for example, 'volunteered' to send us less of her cheap video recorders, compact disc players and colour televisions since they were hurting our home manufacturers. But then, South Korea needs our 'protection' from North Korea.

Some things can just simply be made far too cheaply in the Third World. Take shoes, for instance. You know how cheaply those millions of Chinese workers can make shoes? If France, Italy and Ireland didn't put quotas on the number of Asian shoes that are allowed in, their fashion industry would be in the dumps.

The production of clothing and textiles has been the entry into manufacturing for many developing countries, because they use simple technology and a great deal of labour. All those busy little Asian hands could out-sew us in a minute. Our designers would be naked in the streets. Textiles and clothing is still Europe's number one manufacturing industry.

The Multi-Fibre Arrangement (MFA) restricts clothing and textile exports from developing countries such as Bangladesh and the Philippines, but not from rich industrialised
countries like the USA. The poor countries don't like it, but what choice do they have?
We've wrapped them up in a labyrinth of regulations. There are 368 quotas, covering 17
Least Developed Countries and 5 East European economies.

As a result of British, French and American import restrictions in the mid-1980s, more
than a half of the shirt factories in Bangladesh, one of the world's poorest countries, had
to close, making redundant many poor women with families to feed.

The abolition of the Multi-Fibre Arrangement would create 20 to 45% more jobs in the
clothing and textile industries in developing countries. Earnings would go up by several
billion US dollars every year.

The MFA is supposed to go out of existence by the year 2003. By that time, the EU will
have given $18 billion in subsidies to its Southern member-states to restructure their tex-
tile and clothing industries so they can compete with Third World producers.

The MFA has worked like a dream! A European dream, that is... In 1985 only 18% of the
clothing and 5% of the textiles sold in the EU was produced in the developing countries.
The EU remains the largest exporter of textiles and clothing in the world.

So it means that we, consumers in Europe, are paying higher prices for clothing just to
keep the Bangladeshis out.

Sure! Keeping our industries cost money, you know. But we also import clothing from the Third World countries, so we can get access to their markets in other areas of trade.

And we are also paying subsidy money to our manufacturers through our taxes? 18 billion?

Here's how it works: A female homeworker in, let's say, the Philippines, gets US$2 to make one blouse. Her costs are $1, so she earns $1 for the blouse. The blouse returns to the sweatshop to be finished, with buttonholes, ironing etc.

The sweatshop owner gets $7 a blouse ($1.25 profit) from the trader who sends it to Europe. The trader sells the blouse to the large retail firm, C&A, for $15. His costs for design, cutting, transport, storage etc. are around $11.50, which leaves him a profit of $3.50 per blouse.

**Profit on clothing by different producers in US dollars**

|  | price | profit | number | total profit |
|---|---|---|---|---|
| homeworker | 2.00 | 0.95 | 50 | 95 |
| sweatshop | 7.00 | 1.25 | 2.000 | 5.000 |
| middleman | 15.00 | 3.50 | 10.000 | 70.000 |
| C&A | 25.00 | 9.00 | 10.000 | 180.000 |

## The Common Agricultural Policy

*Another great protection device we have is the Common Agricultural Policy, CAP. Agriculture, the main export sector for most industrialised countries, including America and Japan, is probably the most protected.*

*The most important export of the Netherlands, one of the highly industrialised countries in the world is ....*

*THE TOMATO !*

*A fragile product, huh?*

*And we protect it!*

Agricultural products from outside the Single European Market face tariffs, quotas and other trade walls. And European farmers receive guaranteed prices for their output.

*The European Union spends more subsidising one cow each year than a farmer in the Third World makes in that year.*

*We're fond of animals.*

After World War II, the EU set up its Common Agricultural Policy in order to become as self sufficient in food production as possible. Farmers in the member-states were given subsidies to boost food production. Cheaper food imports from outside the EU faced levies, quotas and other restrictions. The result was the creation of huge food surpluses which, with high EU export subsidies, were dumped on non-EU markets, local farmers in developing countries can no longer compete. They stop farming and migrate to urban areas in search of non-existent jobs.

Some half of the total budget of the European Union is spent on agriculture. Taxpayers in the EU member states finance these budgets.

And because of the high prices for grain in the EU, cattle farmers there import feed from Africa (the Sahel region) or Asia (tapioca from Thailand). This ties up fertile land in developing countries for the production of cattle feed for the North, instead of food production for local markets in the South. The soil becomes eroded there, while the intensive cattle breeding in Europe creates manure surpluses that damage the environment.

The biggest battle over agriculture is between two of the great industrialised powers in the world: the European Union and the USA, but recently an agreement was reached.

But this would seriously endanger the policies of those developing countries who are still trying to set up and maintain their fragile systems of food self-sufficiency. Furthermore quite a number of developing countries have become dependent on the subsidised food exported from Europe and the USA. Now that their local agriculture has been destroyed, their food bills will go skyrocketing.

These are former European colonies and are known as the ACP countries (African, Caribbean and Pacific states). They include some of the poorest countries in the world. Somalia, for example. Europe has signed something called the Lome Convention with them. In principle, 99% of their industrial goods can enter Europe without being taxed.

And sorghum and rice. Sorghum and rice face tariffs... and quotas tied up with tariffs. Fruit and vegetables can only enter the EU in the winter, when the EU cannot produce fruit and vegetables cheaply.

In fact, the ACP countries can only export 10 products to the EU, all of them raw materials like bauxite, copper, coffee, cocoa, bananas, sugar and copra.

Cheap raw materials are an important means of reducing European costs of production. African workers in copper, iron ore and coal mines provide them for rock-bottom wages. African farmers and peasants turn into producers of 'cash crops', i.e. producers of primary agricultural commodities for export, instead of growing healthy food they can eat.

Other Third World countries are also being given 'Preferential Treatment'. These are the Maghreb and Mashreq countries in Northern Africa and the Middle East.

Then, help is being extended to East European countries and the developing countries who are not in the ACP group. They enjoy the conditions of the so-called Generalised System of Preferences, GSP.

## The Generalised System of Preferences

This system, the GSP, lists a range of mainly industrial and semi-manufactured products from developing countries which enjoy preferential treatment—mainly exemption from duties- when they enter Europe. But it excludes basic agricultural products, basic industrial products and raw materials for industry. All manufactured products now fall into four categories depending on how far they compete with local products: very sensitive, sensitive, semi-sensitive and non-sensitive. Only non-sensitive products now enter the European Union duty-free.

Hah! But the many crucial exceptions particularly affect those goods which Third World countries can produce in the early stages of industrialisation. For example: fresh pineapples attract a duty of some 9%, canned pineapples 32% and pineapple juice 42%.

What does all this help add up to?

Non-tariff barriers have completely eroded the advantages of preferential treatment. The share of raw materials from the Third World in the imports of the European Union has gone down from 28% to 18% between 1981-1988.

The governments of the European Union, USA and Japan have dominated the playing field of international trade negotiations during the last decades. Then, production and trade flows worldwide are controlled by a small number of transnational corporations. At least 40% of total world trade takes place outside any market system. This so-called intra-firm trade between companies enables them to set prices themselves and manipulate profits without any control of governments, unions or international institutions.

The majority of developing countries have lost their agricultural and economic independence. They have become suppliers of raw materials for rich consumer markets in the North. World prices for their commodities have dropped significantly. In the ACP countries commodity prices dropped some 37% between 1980 and 1987.

## A Peep into the Future

And you're going to save us money! Synthetic materials and substitutes for agricultural raw materials, made through bio-technology, have led to the decline—from around 20% in 1980 to around 10% in 1987—of the Third World countries' share of Europe's imports.

And on top of the General EU Protectionism...

Each EU member state also uses its national powers to protect itself. For example, in Holland, 49% of the clothing sold comes from developing countries. But in Italy, which has its own domestic clothing industry, the figure is 4%. The Belgians import 31% of their shoes from developing countries, the Italians only 3%. For chemical products, Italy is no. 1 in opening up 4% of its market for Third World imports, while West Germany is last by offering only 2%.

# Standards
The Standoffish Way to deal with Third World Imports

There are different national standards relating to health, safety, environmental and national security. This creates problems for developing countries concerning their exports of meat, fish and plants. They often don't know what standard to choose. Besides EU-wide checks and investigations, on-the-spot bureaucratic harassment by customs officials can be increased.

When the standards are harmonised, a high minimum level will be chosen. Less developed countries will find it difficult to meet these standards. The greatest of such problems will be over fish and fish products. The new EU directive on toy safety will affect south-east Asian exporters. Tobacco growers in Zimbabwe will have to adapt to low-tar standards. Togo and Senegal need to limit cadmium residues in fertilisers, otherwise their fruit exports to the EU will be blocked.

The Third World needs technical and financial support to improve their quality control systems and the quality of their products, as well as punctual and up-to-date information from the EU itself.

Standards on chocolate imports, for example, will affect exporters of cocoa. All member states of the European Union require a minimum percentage of cocoa butter in their chocolate products. But Cadbury and Mars in the UK are now producing chocolate from palm oil.

Soon, non-cocoa may sweep EU markets, and sweep away the earnings of Third World cocoa growers.

New directives From the Centre of the European Union's Decision-Makers: Brussels!

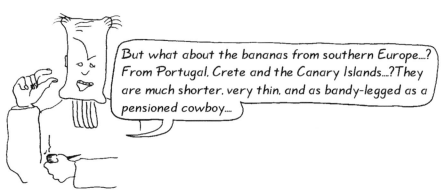

Then there are the different levels of taxation. Germany, for instance, taxes coffee and tea at over 50%. Cocoa is also taxed in the EU member states. Reducing these tax rates will augment world market prices and boost EU import volumes. However, consumers won't suddenly drink much more cups of coffee or tea and eat twice as much chocolate as they do today... And lower prices are often only partially passed on by wholesalers and retailers to the consumer—or not passed on at all.

And then, let us not forget that 'Europe is for the Europeans'. The competitive thrust of the Single European Market is particularly aimed at strengthening Europe's corporations vis-a-vis the USA and Japan. The Single European Market encourages restructuring and Euro-mergers, even though the subsequent 'rationalisations' threaten huge job losses. This will create economic and social stress, which will decrease any existing willingness to give a 'helping hand' to the poor in the Third World.

# CHAPTER 3

# **Whodunnit?**

## Who made these Arrangements?

The European Union was set up precisely to strengthen European trading power. If each country's companies, it was thought, can sell its products in other countries in Europe, their markets will expand and they will have more room to grow rich.

But for this to work effectively, there needed to be a monetary union, in which the currencies of the different member states were harmonised and stabilised. Thus, over the last years, there has been a great deal of economic harmonisation.

In the future, no country will belong to the EU if its budget deficit is over 3% of its GNP (Gross National Product), its inflation more than 4%, or its state debt above 60% of GNP. At the moment, only very few member states are in that position. Even a wealthy nation like the Netherlands isn't. There will therefore have to be tax increases and severe cuts in national government spending, mostly on education, health care and social security in all member states.

There also needs to be a great deal of political harmonisation. All the countries have to be equally stable. Foreign and security policies have to be made in common. This requires cooperation on internal and legal affairs, which includes social affairs (though Great Britain has opted out of this requirement).

Who is this European Union that is Imposing All these Cuts and Hardships?
Well, that will take some time to explain.
The European Union's policies are made by the European Commission, which contains 20 members (or Commissioners), who are supposed to act independently of the interests of the countries where they originate.

*A European Commissioner:*

Headed by a President, the Commission makes proposals on specific issues, which are then implemented by 'Directorate Generals' (DGs) who each deal with a specific area of EU policy. DG VIII is charged with development cooperation with the ACP countries.

But then there is the Council of Ministers, which claims to have the main decision-making power. It is made up of representatives of the governments of the member states. All member states of the European Union send one or more representatives—as a rule, though not necessarily, the minister or secretary of state responsible for the issue being debated, for example foreign affairs, economic affairs, finance, labour, agriculture, transport, technology etc.

Then there is also the European Council, which makes decisions on foreign and security matters, and is made up of the Heads of Government and the President of the Commission, assisted by the Foreign Ministers and a Member of the Commission. Their meetings have become known as European summit meetings. They try to resolve issues which are deadlocked in the Council of Ministers.

Well, there is the European Parliament. It's members (more than 600) are elected directly by the people of the member-states. It has very limited—but growing—powers: the Maastricht Treaty grants it a 'co-decision' right, a sort of veto-right, covering limited policy areas.

The European Parliament is, above all, a platform for debate through which pressure is exerted on the European Commission and the member states.

Together the Council of Ministers and the European Parliament form the budgetary authority with the Parliament playing an important role in the adoption and implementation of the Community budget. On 'compulsory' expenditure (mainly agriculture), the Council of Ministers has the final word. But for other types of expenditures the final decisions rest with the European Parliament.

However it is the European Council or the Council of Ministers that takes all vital decisions, on an inter-governmental level: straight between governments themselves.

# The European Union and Migration

Migrants, Refugees, Asylum-seekers:
If my Goods can't enter Europe, can I?

Imagine a shack somewhere in Africa with a family of eight living on minimum wage. Daily life means only one meal a day, no money for medicines and daily violence by soldiers.

These soldiers are hired by the ruling elite with the revenues from trading coffee or cocoa to the EU and other prosperous markets in the North. For the sake of our daily cup of coffee, our governments maintain good economic relationships with governments in the South, no matter how much they ill-treat their citizens.

Obviously, the inhabitants of our shack would try to move if they can: to places where they can make a better living and not be brutalised by those with power. They want to be free. And they hear that there's freedom in Europe.

But does this apply to the eight million non-EU citizens who live in Europe? No. They have second class status. And those outside the European walls face increasingly stringent barriers. These decisions have been made behind closed doors. Negotiations and agreements that directly affect the position of immigrant workers, asylum-seekers and refugees in and outside the EU are taking place between high-ranking bureaucrats and politicians, who make deals on an inter-governmental level, which means no direct democratic control is involved.

In a wide range of inter-governmental bodies and committees the politicians and bureaucrats take measures to control migration into Europe. Immigration and refugee matters are often treated as part of border controls and of combating criminality. Non-EU citizens are not represented at these inter-governmental negotiations, nor are the European Parliament or the European Court of Justice. National parliaments can only approve or reject treaties cooked up at an inter-governmental level, by, for example:

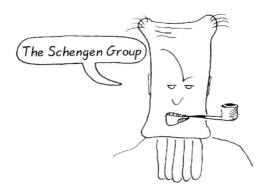

The inter-governmental body consisting of France, Germany, Belgium, Luxembourg, the Netherlands, Spain and Portugal. Almost everybody, in fact.

On 26 March 1995, the borders between France, Germany, the Benelux countries, Spain and Portugal, ceased to exist for EU citizens who travel between these countries. Greece and Italy intend to join this group when they have installed the requisite computer equipment. Denmark, Sweden and Finland are staying outside it temporarily for domestic logistical reasons. Austria wants to join. Britain, however, has made clear that it wants nothing to do with any reduction of border controls and Ireland has to be dragged along in this decision for geographical reasons.

The European Parliament as well as the European Court of Justice were kept ignorant about its content. National parliaments were forced to 'take-it-or-leave-it'. Lawyers have objected strongly to it. It did not standardise policies, but merely co-ordinated their deportation and protection measures.

## The TREVI-Group

This inter-governmental body which consists of the ministers of Internal Affairs and of Justice, was set up in 1975 to coordinate anti-terrorist measures. It is now extended to fighting internationally organised crime and drug trafficking.

They proposed to set up a European Police Bureau like the US-based Federal Bureau of Investigation, FBI. In 1991 the EU member states decided to create Europol, which will collect and analyse data on cross border crime, and be connected with the Schengen Information System.

The TREVI Group does not officially deal with asylum seekers or refugees but, as they are to control 'aliens', their activities will directly affect asylum seekers and refugees.

## The Ad Hoc Immigration Group

This group consists of senior civil servants of the ministries of Internal Affairs or Justice who deal with immigration affairs in the member states. This group drafted the Dublin Convention which determines the state responsible for dealing with a request for asylum tabled in one of the EU member states. It also makes concrete proposals on the conditions under which asylum applications can be rejected as manifestly unfounded applications, and on defining the country of first asylum to which the rejected asylum seekers can be returned. A clearinghouse will be set up to gather and exchange information on asylum matters, such as the situation in the home countries and national law of precedent, more specifically jurisprudence on asylum determination procedures.

It was agreed in the Maastricht Treaty that all EU member states will take major decisions about immigration matters jointly on an intergovernmental level. Intergovernmental means that not only is the European Commission excluded from any involvement in this area of responsibility, but the national parliaments of the member states and the European Parliament are prevented from exercising any overview or democratic control over the decision-making process in the Council of Ministers. The principal role is given to a newly created Council of Justice and Interior Ministers. But real power will lie with a committee of senior officials comprising the so-called K4 Committee, a new bureaucracy being designed to replace the TREVI and Ad Hoc groups. The membership of the K4 Committee is secret, as are its deliberations, although it is known to comprise one representative from each member state plus an official from the European Commission.

There have been some extensions made for the European Parliament on, for example, co-decision-making powers regarding free movement of workers, and mere consultancy status with regard to entry and residence of non-EU nationals.

Under the Maastricht Treaty, citizens of an EU member state are entitled to vote and are eligible for election.

In cases of emergencies the Council of Ministers of the European Union may require visas for a period of six months, without consulting the European Parliament.

All rule-making and decision-making is taking place on an inter-governmental level so EU bodies such as the European Parliament and the European Court of Justice have no real say over asylum and migration policies.

Following the creation of the European Economic Area, the European Union has strengthened its ties with Switzerland, Norway, Iceland and Liechtenstein.

## What Effects will these Treaties have for Non-Europeans?

So the net effect is more intensive controls, varying from street surveillance to cross-border linkages of data from registration systems.

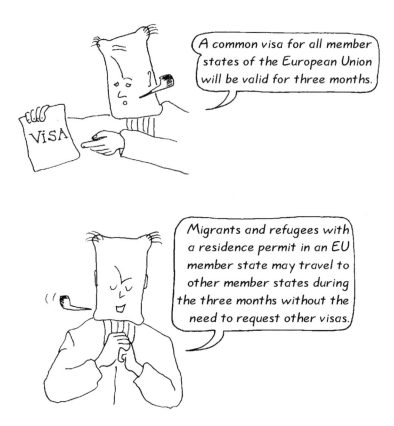

But it will be tougher to enter the European Union. An entry visa can only be obtained at EU embassies in home countries, and no longer at the EU member states' external frontiers. The non-EU citizen should have valid travel documents and prove sufficient means of income, should not be on a national list of non-admissible persons etc.

Such information is compiled in electronic data banks. Through the Schengen Information System, SIS, data concerning refugees whose applications have been rejected, their deportation and the prevention of re-entry is being centralised in a custom-built bunker in the suburbs of Strasbourg. Police computers in each signatory country are linked to the Strasbourg bunker: Germany alone has 8,000 computers linked to SIS. The system has a database capacity of seven to eight million items, including entries on 700,000 individuals. These individuals consist of criminals and other 'undesirables', refugees, asylumseekers and individuals under surveillance both within and outside the European Union.

Under the Schengen Treaty an alien who is to be expelled will be expelled from the whole Schengen territory.

And the 'Schengen countries' will keep their eyes on one another because once accepted by one country the asylum seeker may settle in any of the other countries that signed the Schengen treaty.

The big change is mainly that if one EU member state decides that the person involved does not meet one of the conditions for entry, all other EU members must also refuse that person entry.

Migrants and refugees of non-EU nationality living in an EU member state have no right to work or settle in another member state, unless they are related to an EU citizen through family ties.

Asylum seekers now have only one opportunity to request asylum. And only one member state is responsible for dealing with the application.

However the measure contradicts the Refugee Treaty of Geneva which says that each individual country should take a decision concerning a request for asylum. And 'Schengen' is not a country.

As a consequence of the Schengen Treaty, each EU member state is very busy avoiding becoming the most 'attractive' member state for asylum. France will, for example, send back an asylum seeker to Germany if it suspects that the person has already been in that country. Thus Germany is made responsible for the asylum application.

In practice the result is stricter criteria for asylum seekers in all member states of the European Union.

The Schengen Treaty, the Dublin Convention and the Convention of the EU member states on the crossing of their external borders will therefore greatly restrict the rights of asylum seekers.

Furthermore, there is no independent, authorised court of appeal to consider decisions taken on the basis of these treaties and conventions.

The elimination of internal borders between member states of the European Union does not mean fewer border controls.

Quite the contrary. There is to be more intensive controls at the external borders of the EU, at airports and seaports. Mobile police brigades are already operating just a few miles behind what once was the border crossing, and setting up refugee centres nearby.

But beyond this, the Schengen Treaty also turns air, sea and land carriers into frontier guards. Whether you look suspicious or not, staff of sea, coach and airline companies can stop you and send you back.

## TOURIST AGENCY THE SINKING SUN

Air, sea and land carriers are being made responsible for non-EU citizens who are refused entry. They have to return the alien to the Third State from which he was transported or to the country that issued her/his travel document, or face penalties as well as having to pay the costs of lodging the alien while he/she is in Europe sending him/her back.
Strong objections have again come from lawyers and from the United Nations High Commissioner for Refugees, UNHCR.

The Schengen countries plus the other EU members states are preparing agreements with non-EU countries to oblige them to take back all illegal persons, both their own nationals and all other persons who traversed a non-EU country to cross the external borders of the European Union. An agreement has already been made with Poland. Other East European countries are to follow.

Also the number of countries where one needs a visa to enter the European Union has been increased. This is to cover people coming from 'critical' regions where refugee movements can be expected. Here again the first barrier for the refugee is already created in the home country.

Now what has the trade policy of European Union and its member states got to do with its migration policy?

When the European Union continues to maintain its trade barriers, which impede economic and social development in those regions where migrants come from, the pressure of migration from outside the European Union will never decrease....

Migration in itself is not the problem.

The unequal worldwide distribution of wealth is.

# CHAPTER 5

# Help! What Next?
## Recommendations

We started this book with the dialogue:

I sell, you buy.
You sell, I buy.

This conversation suggests a direct contact between the producer and consumer on the spot. But in reality, today's producer and consumer never meet in the market.

All that happens in between has increasingly become the sole territory of creatures who are known as middlemen, brokers, international firms and, last but not least, (supra)national governments.

Consumers know very little about the conditions of life and work of those producing the goods and services they use. Do they earn enough to make a living? How much do women—who, worldwide, make up the majority of producers—share in the rewards of production? Under what conditions do workers, men, women and often children, produce for middlemen, firms, brokers etc.?

The question after reading this book—what next?—is already partly being answered by a change in the orthodox, unequal trade pattern: the movement for Fair Trade.

There are already lots of initiatives: the setting up of alternative trade organisations for the distribution of fair trade products, such as Max Havelaar Coffee, Cafe Direct, and other products, chocolate, bananas etc. In addition, there are also so-called social venture networks or companies who have established their own codes of conduct dealing with working conditions, labour standards, the environment.

But the entire idea is not to juggle with 'alternatives' to compete with the mainstream trade in goods and services. The idea is to work towards changes in the system itself, not only as consumers, but as political actors, who vote for the people making the decisions. There are ways to do this.

At the beginning of this book we noted that the Maastricht Treaty states:
"The Community shall take account of the objectives referred to in Article 130u in the policies that it implements which are likely to affect developing countries".
Article 130u covers the following:
1    "Community policy in the sphere of development cooperation which shall be complementary to the policies pursued by the Member States, shall foster:
  – the sustainable economic and social development of developing countries, and more particularly the most disadvantaged among them;
  – the smooth and gradual integration of developing countries into the world economy;
  – the campaign against poverty in developing countries."

2    "Community policy in this area shall contribute to the general objective of developing and consolidating democracy and the rule of law, and shall respect human rights and fundamental freedoms."

There is therefore a legal basis for asking whether 95% of Europe's policies, which are not development cooperation but affect developing countries, are consistent with the objectives of development cooperation.

Does the Common Agricultural Policy undermine agricultural production in developing countries? Does European trade policy hinder the emergence of manufacturing in poorer parts of the world?

There are no guarantees built into the Maastricht Treaty that Article 130u will be respected. But it does offer organisations and groups an instrument for campaigning on trade and migration issues from the perspective of a more just Europe. It also provides a basis for the European Parliament to challenge the lack of coherence in the EU's trade and agriculture policies.

## Recommendations for Lobbying

1   For a direct halt to the dumping of agricultural products on developing countries' markets.
2   The removal of import tariffs on products from developing countries.
3   The banning of arms exports to countries where there are conflicts.
The release of information to the consumer, not only on the contents of products, but also on the makers of products: conditions of life and work, wages, and effects on the environment.

## Recommendations for Campaigns

You can join us and take ACTION! In almost every member state of the European Union, non-governmental organisations, trade unions, third world support groups, human rights organisations, consumer groups and environmentalists are promoting fair trade and social justice campaigns on a range of issues. There are, for example,campaigns on "clean" clothes, "clean" sports shoes and sportswear, toys, soccers balls and floor rugs. There are fair trade campaigns on coffee, tea and banana's. Work is being done to press multinationals, including Nike, Reebok, C&A, Shell and others, to accept fair trade charters and codes of conduct to improve social and environmental conditions at the workplace. There are campaigns to fight racism, xenophobia and to support migrants, refugees and people seeking asylum.
DO IT! JOIN IN!

# About IRENE

If you want to have information about the organisations and groups in Europe and abroad that run campaigns, do research and lobbying and organize workshops on commodities, fair trade and on the rights of migrants, refugees and asylum-seekers, contact:

IRENE
International Restructuring Education Network Europe
Stationsstraat 39
5038 EC Tilburg
The Netherlands
tel: + 31.13.535.15.23.
fax: + 31.13.535.02.53.
E-mail: irene@antenna.nl

*Peter Pennartz* is an economist specialising in labour relations. He is currently working with the International Restructuring Education Network Europe (IRENE), an international NGO based in The Netherlands which has a training and education programme on international restructuring in industries and services. He also acts as a consultant and has been working on the labour sector in South Africa.